Selected & New Poems

Selected & New Poems

Michael Hartnett

Edited by Peter Fallon

WAKE FOREST UNIVERSITY PRESS

Published in America by Wake Forest University Press in 1994. Text
designed by Peter Fallon and published in Britain and Ireland by the
Gallery Press in 1994.

ISBN   0-916390-62-4
LC Card Number 94-60357

Contents

'Whom I ask for no gift . . .' *page* 11

A Small Farm 13
'There will be a talking . . .' 14
'I heard him whistle . . .' 15
For My Grandmother, Bridget Halpin 16
Bread 17
Sad Singing in Darkness 18
'I have exhausted the delighted range . . .' 19
Sickroom 20
Green Room 21
Prayer at Death 22
Anatomy of a Cliché
   1 mo ghrá thú 23
   2 'Some white academy of grace . . .' 24
   3 'Listen . . .' 25
Notes on My Contemporaries
   1 The Poet Down 26
   2 The Poet as Mastercraftsman 27
   3 The Poet as Black Sheep 28
   4 The Person as Dreamer: We Talk About the Future 29
   5 The Poet Dreams and Resolves 30
Prisoners 31
The Retreat of Ita Cagney 33
from Thirteen Sonnets
   1 'I have been stone, dust of space, sea and sphere . . .' 40
   9 'I saw magic on a green country road . . .' 41
Lament for Tadhg Cronin's Children 42
The Oatwoman 43
A Visit to Castletown House 45
Death of an Irishwoman 47
That Actor Kiss 48
A Visit to Croom, 1745 49
from A Farewell to English 50
The Last Vision of Eoghan Rua Ó Súilleabháin 52

The Wounded Otter 53
Poem for Lara, 10 54
The Naked Surgeon 55
'Bereft of its great poets . . . ' 67
'Pity the man who English lacks . . . ' 68
Inchicore Haiku 69
No Avail 70
A Falling Out 71
Mountains, Fall on Us 73
The Old Catechism 80
The Man who Wrote Yeats, the Man who Wrote Mozart 84
Sibelius in Silence 91
He'll to the Moors 97

for Angela

Whom I ask for no gift,
whom I thank for all things,
this is the morning.
Night is gone, a dawn
comes up in birds and sounds of the city.
There will be light
to live by, things
to see: my eyes will lift
to where the sun in vermilion sits,
and I will love and have pity.

A Small Farm

All the perversions of the soul
I learnt on a small farm,
how to do the neighbours harm
by magic, how to hate.
I was abandoned to their tragedies,
minor but unhealing:
bitterness over boggy land,
casual stealing of crops,
venomous card games
across swearing tables,
a little music on the road,
a little peace in decrepit stables.
Here were rosary beads,
a bleeding face,
the glinting doors
that did encase
their cutler needs,
their plates, their knives,
the cracked calendars
of their lives.

I was abandoned to their tragedies
and began to count the birds,
to deduce secrets in the kitchen cold,
and to avoid among my nameless weeds
the civil war of that household.

'There will be a talking . . .'

There will be a talking of lovely things,
there will be cognizance of the seasons,
there will be men who know the flights of birds.
In new days there will be love for women:
we will walk the balance of artistry,
and things will have a middle and an end,
and be loved because they are beautiful.
Who in a walk will find a lasting vase
depicting dance and hold it in his hands
and sell it then? No man on the new earth
will barter with malice nor make of stone
a hollowed riddle; for art will be art,
the freak, the rare no longer commonplace.
There will be a going back to the laws.

'I heard him whistle . . .'

I heard him whistle
in the night-frost,
delicate waterbirds,
your otter, meshed
in crochet moss.
I shot him dead —
sudden fire and smoke,
crackles of moonlight
from my rifle,
rain from erupted water
made a small rain back
and the echo batted
along the hills, a ball
on the hollow floor
of an above room.
I sat in the shallows
crying, eating
the vital parts
of a trout:
and with a knife
I slit the skin
between
my webbed fingers.

For My Grandmother, Bridget Halpin

Maybe morning lightens over
the coldest time in all the day,
but not for you. A bird's hover,
seabird, blackbird, or bird of prey,
was rain, or death, or lost cattle.
The day's warning, like red plovers
so etched and small the clouded sky,
was book to you, and true bible.
You died in utter loneliness,
your acres left to the childless.
You never saw the animals
of God, and the flower under
your feet; and the trees change a leaf;
and the red fur of a fox on
a quiet evening; and the long
birches falling down the hillside.

Bread

Her iron beats
the smell of bread
from damp linen,
silver, crystal,
and warm white things.
Whatever bird
I used to be,
hawk or lapwing,
tern, or something
wild, fierce or shy,
these birds are dead,
and I come here
on tiring wings.
Odours of bread . . .

Sad Singing in Darkness

Sad singing in darkness is our burden
for we have none to look to or to love.
We are lovers of rare earth; our plots
are few but flourish in the sunless angles.
No one alien for us: we have pools
to tell us who and the lipsound of stones
breaking the water is prelude to the form
that is our love. Long we gaze upon the pools,
the terrible swaying of the water:
for in these undulations is the face . . .

1958

'I have exhausted the delighted range . . .'

I have exhausted the delighted range
of small birds, and now, a new end to pain
makes a mirage of what I wished my life.
Torture, immediate to me, is strange;
all that is left of the organs remain
in an anaesthetic of unbelief.

Coerced by trivia, nothing to gain
but now, or to be pleased through one long night

and forsake instead something immortal?
And the graceless heron is killed in flight
and falls like a lopped flower into the stalks.

Small birds, small poems, are not immortal,
nor, however passed, is one intense night:
there is no time now for my dream of hawks.

Sickroom

Regularly I visited,
since your sickness,
you in the black bedroom
with the gauze of death
around you like your sheets.

Now I must be frank:
these are not roses beside you,
   nor are these grapes,
      and this is no portrait
         of your father's friend.

I know you cannot rise.
You are unable to move.
But I can see your fear,
for two wet mice
         dart
cornered in the hollows
of your head.

Green Room

This cell we keep unlocked,
for here is a gentle man tending ferns,
to whom there is no world
but the mute fern world,
where all is green and delicate
and there is no strife,
save the stems thrusting at the earth
the spore being loosed on the air
in silence, and coming to ground
as silently . . . .
We do not allow him a trowel:
you notice he breaks the loam
with his fingers.
Do not attempt conversation:
he will ignore you.
There is no voice for him
but the fern-arms gentling to the window.
It is so foamed with green lace here
that we call his room
'the green tapestried room'.

Prayer at Death

What was not human
though from womb of woman,
for this, a small grief.
For this, who forced a love
on you, will have to be
the necessary funeral,
the necessary grief.
For you, already
skeletal, you have sinned
by forcing years of faithfulness from us,
die now, rest: let us rest.

There will be valid
human grief for all
these deaths: the heart will love
all it has to love.

Anatomy of a Cliché

1 *mo ghrá thú*

With me, so you call me man.
Stay: winter is harsh to us,
my self is worth no money.
But with your self spread over
me, eggs under woodcock-wings,
the grass will not be meagre:
where we walk will be white flowers.

So rare will my flesh cry out
I will not call at strange times.
We will couple when you wish:
for your womb estranges death.
Jail me in this gentle land;
let your hands hold me: I am
not man until less than man.

2

Some white academy of grace
taught her to dance in perfect ways:
neck, as locked lily, is not wan
on this great, undulating bird.

Are they indeed your soul, those hands,
as frantic as lace in a wind,
forever unable to fly
from the beauty of your body?

And if they dance, your five white fawns,
walking lawns of your spoken word,
what may I do but let linger
my eyes on each luminous bone?

Your hands . . . are music and phrases
escape your fingers as they move,
and make the unmappable lands
quiet orchestra of your limbs.

For I have seen your hands in fields
and I called them fluted flowers
such as the lily is, before
it unleashes its starwhite life:

I have seen your fingernail cut
the sky and called it the new moon . . . .

3

Listen,
if I came to you, out of the wind
with only my blown dream clothing me,
would you give me shelter?
For I have nothing —
or nothing the world wants.
I love you: that is all my fortune.

But I know we cannot sail without nets:
I know you cannot be exposed
however soft the wind
or however small the rain.

Notes on My Contemporaries

1 *The Poet Down*

for Patrick Kavanagh

He sits between the doctor and the law.
Neither can help. Barbiturate in paw
one, whiskey in paw two, a dying man:
the poet down, and his fell caravan.
They laugh and they mistake the lash that lurks
in his tongue for the honey of his works.
The poet is at bay, the hounds baying,
dig his grave with careful kindness, saying:
'Another whiskey, and make it a large one!'
Priests within, acolytes at the margin
the red impaled bull's roar must fascinate —
they love the dead, the living man they hate.
They were designing monuments — in case —
and making furtive sketches of his face,
and he could hear, above their straining laughs,
the rustling foolscap of their epitaphs.

2 The Poet as Mastercraftsman

for Thomas Kinsella

Eras do not end when great poets die,
for poetry is not whole, it is where man
chose mountains to conform, to carve his own
face among the Gothic richness and the sky,
and the gargoyles, and the lesser tradesmen.
Praise from the apprentice is always shown
in miniatures of a similar stone.
I saw the master in his human guise
open doors to let me in, and rhythm out.
He smiled and entertained into the night.
I was aware of work undone. His eyes,
like owls', warned images from the room.
Under the stairs the muse was crying; shields
clashed in the kitchen and the war drum's boom,
men in celtic war dress entered from the right.
I left, my conversation put to rout.

To poets peace poetry never yields.

3 *The Poet as Black Sheep*

for Paul Durcan

I have seen him dine
in middle-class surroundings,
his manners refined,
as his family around him
talk about nothing,
one of their favourite theses.

I have seen him lying
between the street and pavement,
atoning, dying
for their sins, the fittest payment
he can make for them,
to get drunk and go to pieces.

On his father's face
in sparse lines etched out by ice,
the puritan race
has come to its zenith of grey spite,
its climax of hate,
its essence of frigidity.

Let the bourgeoisie beware,
who could not control his head
and kept it in their care
until the brain bled:
this head is a poet's head,
this head holds a galaxy.

4 *The Person as Dreamer: We Talk about the Future*

for Des Healy

It has to be a hill,
high, of course, and twilit.
There have to be some birds,
all sadly audible:
a necessary haze,
and small wristlets of rain,
yes, and a tremendous
air of satisfaction.
Both of us will be old
and both our wives, of course,
have died, young, and tragic.
And all our children have
gone their far ways, estranged,
or else not begotten.
We have been through a war,
been hungry, and heroes:
and here we are now, calm,
fed, and reminiscent.
The hills are old, silent:
our pipe-smoke rises up.
We have come a long way . . . .

5 *The Poet Dreams and Resolves*

for Macdara Woods.

To be alone, and not to be lonely,
to have time to myself, and not be bored;
to live in some suburban house, beside
the mountains, with an adequate supply
of stout and spirits (or of stout only),
and some cigarettes, and writing paper,
and a little cheap food, and a small hoard
of necessary books, where I could write
in dark as monks did, with only blue sky
as interference, wind as soul-reaper.

But what would I do if on certain nights
I was mad in heat for the public lights?
I would chain myself to a living tree
to foil the Sirens of the distant city.

Prisoners

Brave
to keep as captive
one he loved, this wild woman
not so old, so many years
in quiet place,
unknown to all the town.
So her face was white as almond
pale as wax for lack of sunlight
blue skin by her eyes in etchings,
all her beauty now attainted,
all her loveliness unwanted.
   Not to say his love was lessened,
   no. He came home to her same altar
   at night, grey horse bore him to the threshold,
   quiet rooms, where the woman sang her service,
   sang to new gods, to the church of her invention
   her own cloistered psalms, in her bishoped dress of scarlet.
For she built walls to keep God in,
and waiting there from eyes ahide
at night before her tearful face
at calm crossroads her child did raise,
her child into the secret world.
   And she involved a secret Lord,
   prayed the holy prayers she made herself,
   and sang so: my Lord God is a human Lord,
   not Lord of towns, but Lord of white horses, holy
   of the hyacinth, the human Lord of light, of rain.
Yes, Lord of sacred anguish, hear
me, and speak in rain of trees: send
your holy fire to heat me. I
cry: my Lord of holy pain, hear.
   House of slated roof was their house,
   daylight knew no way to hound them
      out of peace:
   the door was closed with iron chains

locked safe inside an open moat
      of water;
secret in their love they lived there:
the birch-hid dove was silk with peace.

The Retreat of Ita Cagney

for Liam Brady

1

Their barbarism did not assuage the grief:
their polished boots, their Sunday clothes,
the drone of hoarse melodeons.
The smoke was like the edge of blue scythes.
The downpour smell of overcoats
made the kitchen cry for air;
snuff lashed the nose like nettles
and the toothless praising of the dead
spun on like unoiled bellows.
She could not understand her grief:
the women who had washed his corpse
were now more intimate with him
than she had ever been.
She put a square of silk upon her head
and hidden in the collars of her coat
she felt her way along the whitewashed walls.
The road became a dim knife.
She had no plan
but instinct neighed around her
like a pulling horse.

2

Moulded to a wedge of jet
by the wet night, her black hair
showed one grey rib, like a fine
steel filing on a forge floor.
One deep line, cut by silent
days of hate in the expanse

of sallow skin above her brows,
dipped down to a tragic slant.
Her eyebrows were thin penlines
finely drawn on parchment sheets,
hair after miniscule hair
a linear masterpiece.
Triangles of minute gold
broke her open blue of eyes
that had looked on bespoke love
seeing only to despise.

Her long nose was almost bone
making her face too severe:
the tight and rose-edged nostrils
never belled into a flare.
A fine gold down above the
upper lip did not maintain
its prettiness nor lower's swell
make it less a graph of pain.
Chin and jawline delicate,
neither weak nor skeletal:
bone in definite stern mould,
small and strong like a fox-skull.
Her throat showed no signs of age.
No sinews reinforced flesh
or gathered in clenched fistfuls
to pull skin to a lined mesh.

The rest was shapeless, in black woollen dress.

3

Door opened halving darkness bronze
and half an outlined man
filled half the bronze.
Lamplight whipped upright into gold
the hairs along his nose,
flowed coils of honey
around his head.
In the centre of his throat
clipped on his blue-striped shirt
a stud briefly pierced a thorn of light.

The male smell of the kitchen
engulfed her face,
odours of lost gristle
and grease along the wall:
her headscarf laughed a challenge,
its crimson wrinkles crackling.
He knuckled up the wooden latch
and closed the door for many years.

4

Great ceremony later causes pain:
next year in hatred and in grief, the vain
white dress, the bulging priest, the frantic dance,
the vowing and the sickening wishes, land
like careful hammers on a broken hand.
But in this house no sacred text was read.
He offered her some food: they went to bed,
his arm and side a helmet for her head.
This was no furtive country coupling: this
was the ultimate hello, kiss and kiss

exchanged and bodies introduced. Their sin —
to choose so late a moment to begin,
while shamefaced chalice, pyx, ciborium
clanged their giltwrapped anger in the room.

5

The swollen leather creaks
like lost birds
and the edges of her shawl
fringe down into the dark
while glaciers of oilskins drip around her
and musical traces and chafing of harness
and tedious drumming of hooves on the gravel
make her labour pains become
the direct rebuke and pummel of the town.

Withdrawing from her pain
to the nightmare warmth
beneath her shawl
the secret meeting in the dark
becomes a public spectacle
and baleful sextons turn their heads
and sullen shadows mutter hate
and snarl and debate
and shout vague threats of hell.

The crossroads blink their headlamp warning
and break into a rainbow on the shining tar:
the new skull turns in its warm pain,
the new skull pushes towards its morning.

6

O my small and warm creature
with your gold hair and your skin
that smells of milk and apples,
I must always lock you in
where nothing much can happen.
But you will hate these few rooms,
for a dove is bound to come
with leaves and outdoor perfumes:
already the talons drum
a beckoning through the slates,
bringing from the people words
and messages of hate.
Soon the wingbeats of this bird
will whisper down in their dive.
I dread the coming of this dove
for its beak will be a knife
and if you leave armed with my love
they will tell you what you lack.

They will make you wear my life
like a hump upon your back.

7

. . . each footprint being green in the wet grass
in search of mushrooms like white moons of lime,
each hazel ooze of cowdung through the toes,
being warm, and slipping like a floor of silk . . .
but all the windows are in mourning here:
the giant eye gleams like a mucous hill.
She pictured cowslips, then his farmer's face,
and waited in a patient discontent.

A heel of mud fell from his garden boots
embossed with nails and white-hilt shoots of grass,
a hive of hayseeds in the woollen grooves
of meadow coats fell golden on the floor,
and apples with medallions of rust
englobed a thickening cider on the shelf:
and holly on the varnished frames bent in
and curved its cat-sharp fingernails of green.
The rooms became resplendent with these signs.

8

I will put purple crêpe and crimson crêpe
and white crêpe on the shelf
and watch the candles cry
O *salutaris hostia.*
I will light the oil lamp till it burns
like a scarlet apple
and watch the candlegrease
upon the ledges interweave
to ropes of ivory.
I have not insulted God:
I have insulted
crombie coats and lace mantillas,
Sunday best and church collections,
and they declare my life a sinful act:
not because it hurts
the God they say they love —
not because their sins are less —
but because my happiness
is not a public fact.

9

In rhythmic dance the neighbours move
outside the door, become dumb dolls
as venom breaks in strident fragments
on the glass; broken insults clatter
on the slates. The pack retreats,
the instruments of siege withdraw
and skulk into the foothills to regroup.
The houses nudge and mutter through the night
and wait intently for the keep to fall.
She guards her sleeping citizen
and paces the exhausting floor:
on the speaking avenue of stones
she hears the infantry of eyes advance.

from *Thirteen Sonnets*

1

I have been stone, dust of space, sea and sphere:
flamed in the supernova before man
or manmade gods made claim to have shaped me.
I have always been, will always be. I
am a pinch of earth compressed in the span
of a snail-shell: galaxies' energy,
the centre of the sun, the arch of sky.
I became all that all things ever can.
I *will* be here: I have always been here.
Buddha had to walk upon me; my snows
were not so kind, my ice was sharp as grass.
Upon me, even Christ encountered fear:
the nails were mine, the mallet mine, the blows
were mine. I grew the tree that grew the Cross.

9

I saw magic on a green country road —
that old woman, a bag of sticks her load,

blackly down to her thin feet a fringed shawl,
a rosary of bone on her horned hand,
a flight of curlews scribing by her head,
and ashtrees combing with their frills her hair.

Her eyes, wet sunken holes pierced by an awl,
must have deciphered her adoring land:
and curlews, no longer lean birds, instead
become ten scarlet comets in the air.

Some incantation from her canyoned mouth,
Irish, English, blew frost along the ground,
and even though the wind was from the South
the ashleaves froze without an ashleaf sound.

Lament for Tadhg Cronin's Children

That day the sails of the ship were torn
and a fog obscured the lawns.
In the whitewashed house the music stopped.
A spark jumped up at the gables
and the silk quilts on the bed caught fire.
They cry without tears —
their hearts cry —
for the three dead children.

Christ God neglect them not
nor leave them in the ground!

They were ears of corn!
They were apples!
They were three harpstrings!
And now their limbs lie underground
and the black beetle walks across their faces.
I, too, cry without tears —
my heart cries —
for the three dead children.

based on a poem by Aodhagán Ó Rathaille

The Oatwoman

She heard the gates of autumn
    splinter into ash,
grey shock of toppling insects
    as the gate broke down.
Old nails in their nests of rust
    screamed at this swivel;
booted limbs of working men
    walked on her body.
Their coats lay down in sculpture,
    each with a tired dog;
thin blades quaked at blunt whetstones,
    purple barked at blue.
The whetstones drank their water
    and flayed the bright edge.
Each oat like sequin shivered;
    her gold body tensed,
fear lapped across her acre
    in a honey wave
and buckets of still porter
    turned to discs of black.
Iron and stone called warning
    to her shaking ears;
arms enforced a fierce caress,
    brown and blind and bronze.
Sickles drove her back and back
    to a golden wedge;
her hissing beads fell silent
    in dead yellow bands.
Across her waist the reaping
    whipped like silver moons,
wind whistled banked flute laments,
    musical sweat fell.
Animals left in terror,
    pheasant, sparrow, hare

deserting her in anguish,
  crowding from her skirts.
She curled in a golden fear
  on the last headland,
the sad outline of her breasts
  bare through the oatstalks.
Four arms took sickles and swung —
  no single killer:
she vanished from the shorn field
  in that red autumn.

A Visit to Castletown House

for Norah Graham

The avenue was green and long, and green
light pooled under the fernheads; a jade screen
could not let such liquid light in, a sea
at its greenest self could not pretend to be
so emerald. Men had made this landscape
from a mere secreting wood: knuckles bled
and bones broke to make this awning drape
a fitting silk upon its owner's head.

The house was lifted by two pillared wings
out of its bulk of solid chisellings
and flashed across the chestnut-marshalled lawn
a few lit windows on a bullock bawn.
The one-way windows of the empty rooms
reflected meadows, now the haunt
of waterbirds: where hawtrees were in bloom,
and belladonna, a poisonous plant.

A newer gentry in their quaint attire
looked at maps depicting alien shire
and city, town, and fort: they were his seed,
that native who had taken coloured beads
disguised as chandeliers of vulgar glass,
and made a room to suit a tasteless man
— a graceful art come to a sorry pass —
painted like some demented tinker's van.

But the music that was played in there —
that had grace, a nervous grace laid bare,
Tortelier unravelling sonatas
pummelling the instrument that has

the deep luxurious sensual sound,
allowing it no richness, making stars
where moons would be, choosing to expound
music as passionate as guitars.

I went into the calmer, gentler hall
in the wineglassed, chattering interval:
there was the smell of rose and woodsmoke there.
I stepped into the gentler evening air
and saw black figures dancing on the lawn,
Eviction, Droit de Seigneur, Broken Bones,
and heard the crack of ligaments being torn
and smelled the clinging blood upon the stones.

Death of an Irishwoman

Ignorant, in the sense
she ate monotonous food
and thought the world was flat,
and pagan, in the sense
she knew the things that moved
at night were neither dogs nor cats
but *púcas* and darkfaced men,
she nevertheless had fierce pride.
But sentenced in the end
to eat thin diminishing porridge
in a stone-cold kitchen
she clenched her brittle hands
around a world
she could not understand.
I loved her from the day she died.
She was a summer dance at the crossroads.
She was a card game where a nose was broken.
She was a song that nobody sings.
She was a house ransacked by soldiers.
She was a language seldom spoken.
She was a child's purse, full of useless things.

That Actor Kiss

I kissed my father as he lay in bed
in the ward. Nurses walked on soles of sleep
and old men argued with themselves all day.
The seven decades locked inside his head
congealed into a timeless leaking heap,
the painter lost his sense of all but grey.
That actor kiss fell down a shaft too deep
to send back echoes that I would have prized —
'29 was '41 was '84,
all one in his kaleidoscopic eyes
(he willed to me his bitterness and thirst,
his cold ability to close a door).
Later, over a drink, I realised
that was our last kiss and, alas, our first.

died 3 October 1984

A Visit to Croom, 1745

for Séamus Ó Cinnéide

The thatch dripped soot,
the sun was silver
because the sky
from ruts of mud to high blaze
was water.
Whitewashed walls were silver,
limeflakes opened like scissored pages
nesting moss and golds of straw
and russet pools of soot;
windows small as rat holes
shone like frost-filled hoofprints,
the door was charted
by the tracery of vermin.
Five Gaelic faces stopped their talk,
turned from the red of fire
into a cloud of rush-light fumes,
scraped their pewter mugs
across the board and talked about the king.
I had walked a long time
in the mud to hear
an avalanche of turf fall down,
fourteen miles in straw-roped overcoat
passing for Irish all along the road,
now to hear a Gaelic court
talk broken English of an English king.
It was a long way
to come for nothing.

from *A Farewell to English*

5

I say farewell to English verse,
to those I found in English nets:
my Lorca holding out his arms
to love the beauty of his bullets,
Pasternak who outlived Stalin
and died because of lesser beasts;
to all the poets I have loved
from Wyatt to Robert Browning;
to Father Hopkins in his crowded grave
and to our bugbear Mr Yeats
who forced us into exile
on islands of bad verse.

Among my living friends
there is no poet I do not love
although some write
with bitterness in their hearts;
they are one art, our many arts.

Poets with progress
make no peace or pact.
The act of poetry
is a rebel act.

7

This road is not new.
I am not a maker of new things.
I cannot hew
out of the vacuum-cleaner minds
the sense of serving dead kings.

I am nothing new.
I am not a lonely mouth
trying to chew
a niche for culture
in the clergy-cluttered south.

But I will not see
great men go down
who walked in rags
from town to town
finding English a necessary sin,
the perfect language to sell pigs in.

I have made my choice
and leave with little weeping.
I have come with meagre voice
to court the language of my people.

The Last Vision of Eoghan Rua Ó Súilleabháin

The cow of morning spurted
milk-mist on each glen
and the noise of feet came
from the hills' white sides.
I saw like phantoms
my fellow-workers
and instead of spades and shovels
they had roses on their shoulders.

The Wounded Otter

A wounded otter
on a bare rock,
a bolt in her side,
stroking her whiskers,
stroking her webbed feet.

Her ancestors
told her once
that there was a river,
a crystal river,
a waterless bed.

They also said
there were trout there
fat as tree-trunks
and kingfishers
bright as blue spears —
men there without cinders
in their boots,
men without dogs
on leashes.

She did not notice
the world die
nor the sun expire.
She was already
swimming at ease
in the magic crystal river.

Poem for Lara, 10

An ashtree on fire
the hair of your head
coaxing larks
with your sweet voice
in the green grass,
a crowd of daisies
playing with you,
a crowd of rabbits
dancing with you,
the blackbird
with its gold bill
is a jewel for you,
the goldfinch
with its sweetness
is your music.
You are perfume,
you are honey,
a wild strawberry:
even the bees think you
a flower in the field.
Little queen of the land of books,
may you always be thus,
may you ever be free
    from sorrow-chains.

Here's my blessing for you, girl,
and it is no petty grace —
may you have the beauty of your mother's soul
    and the beauty of her face.

The Naked Surgeon

1

The sky is alone tonight —
the moon and stars
seek some presence
in the firm quiet, in the hard lack.
A meteor falls in the empty dark.
Someone is absent, the universe is bare —
listen, God, are you there?

Sand silts the world —
dockleaves in the yard,
broken teeth eat sadness
in the hayless barn.
Silence knocks on men's doors
and silence answers it —
but music is heard in space.

Lichen eats the stone,
old arrogance eats peace:
female salt eats being,
angry rust eats blood.
Beetle and seal are dead,
poisoned children in lakes —
but music is heard in space.

Weak whistle-music moves
beyond Orion's Belt,
silk threads in a cave
float in the dark.
Some player in the solitude
with a hopeful song
but destruction still goes on.

Lard made from whales,
coats from the seals' fur —
shaving brush from badger hair,
burnt chicks are henfood.
God's lovely creatures last
though we eat them, trout and lamb —
there's a use for the whistler's tune.

I saw a nest ablaze,
living wood sawdust.
I saw a bird on fire
fall soundless from the air.
I saw the ancient ramparts downed
and silence in the plover field.
I saw the killer's belly feed.

A tongue hangs on a tree,
the magpies' might is right:
a noise of glossy black and white.
I heard their loud artillery.
My ears are withered leaves
from their cacophony,
the discord shuts God's eyes.
But a new musician plays
and music's heard in space.

2

Listen, father, wait a while —
stay alive with me until
the universe's gown,
once as fresh as cabbage-heart,
is clean again.
Do you remember mothers' milk
like pigeons' milk that feeds the flock?
It will pour again — wait on.

I saw it last night
in the northern sky
whiter than any blood
dripped from the moon's pap
and every parched grave opened up
and the dough of milk and earth
made a bread forever fresh.

Listen, father, listen close —
though the sky's a tambourine
danced on by an iron fool
there's harmony beyond his noise.
Take time and slow your pace —
the dark drink waits for you
and strange music out in space.

Did you see them last night,
night's-eyes brilliant bright
in the black grass
and dandelions *en masse*,
guineas on velvet once
on an old god's shoulders
dead since the ancient magic passed?

Remember the age of the seed,
kingdom of creatures, power of air?
(Man was not alone,
man and his household.)
Waterfall tumbling from eldertree,
foam on pools like feather capes?
Remember pollen from grasses' ears?

Listen, father, cry no tear
for evil seed, for history's débris,
for the cold eternal stones,
ruined towers, groves of graves.
Listen: a bullfinch sings sweetly
(musical anvil in forge)
his harmony's all history.

So, my father, wait a while.
There's no music after dying,
no inkling of a human sigh —
just worlds falling into suns.
Earth will be the brightest bride,
star-necklets on her gown —
tinwhistles cracking tunes,
platform dances in each town.
Easy, father, wait a while.

But he did not wait.

3

One day when hope was ill
I took dangerous medicine
and hope died out and left me there,
a naked surgeon, my patient dead.
Like a hen at grips with death
my bill dumb down a well,
my plumage drowned in hate.

I turned my back on Glendarock,
walked for a drink to ease
and to obliterate
pain and fear and grief.
Rats laughed from every hedge,
bones embossed the road —
in the wind a grey crow screeched.

And then I saw the sign
that led my heart to peace —
barley like a green fire,
sheets of barley in live waves
quivering its thousand ears,
swaying flames of green
as quietly restless as a child asleep.

I knew then no victory
would go to iron axe or spear:
our mother which art on earth
conserve us safe and clean.
Gale and 'quake knock flat
all laws, all walls, all treasuries —
bindweed chokes the telegraph.

In spite of joy this peace waned
and ice ran through every vein:
all my pores were locked
and my heart turned,
a piglet on a spit, his blood steam,
panting like a dog's tongue;
the scythe taught the corn its dream.

Caterpillars squashed on the roads,
the swallow snapping back flies,
frogspawn dead in pools dried up,
the horsefly craving blood.
Prick in a vice, a man screams.
The scythe taught the poet his dream.

Barley, cover me up,
let me lie in your field.
I ask of you a green death
in the quiet milk of your stalks.
Yes, the world will survive
with neither you nor me alive.
Damn you, death, I will not then experience
the new gown of the universe —
just lie manure on immaculate earth.

4

Once a perfect standing stone,
fame engraved on my side,
my statement unambiguous,
I had nothing to hide.
But the wind of curiosity blew
with its *what?* and *how?* and *why?*
and blunted the edge of my dignity.

The cow of love rubbed its flank
against my sides and frost burnt:
the grain inside me shrank,
I flaked on the grass bank.
A flock of questions came seeking food
and the mother in me said 'chook, chook'
though I was dumb and mere rock.

The anxiety mason chipped at me
with his heavy hammer,
carving his own design:
his chisel gouged my grammar,
engraved no notices of mine
and every passing stray has read
words not engendered in my head.

And the lichen letters came
twisting the bare word
and their grey crust grew on me
and concealed my shape.
I lost all courage and desire,
my voice was just a shard
and all the silent world had ears.

My body like a dead elm —
dumb lightning upside-down —
inquisitor's file eroding me,
wedges wearing me out.
Before me, in my mouth,
restraints and oaths — but my poem stayed,
I still stand. But where are they?

The sky stands on my tip,
stars flow through me, inside:
I tame the sun and moon,
harnessed to my pride.
No friendships flourish in my shade,
no herb of love, no mint of help,
and I'm incapable of prayer.

Now merely a lump of stone
smashed in the field of scythes,
a circle of calves around me
staring with silly eyes.
I lonesome like a hawtree
while lichen hones me down
and a lizard-brooch sleeps.

5

In Hammer Glen there's blood
in milk and a goose complains
on an empty hearth: a cat
swells in the churn, dead and full.
A flitch of bacon hangs itself
from rafters: a tongs stands like a bull.
My first trip to the house of thatch —

home of the Slaughter Lad
who condemned his own kind —
a hammer-vision showed him how
to escape the bird-lime.
I was called, no scalpel packed.
I threw a saddle on the dark
and galloped to the threshold of his mind.

Knots of briars slid from their nests,
each poisoned eye a blackberry.
I was pelted with a shower of fruit
from a bare blackthorn tree.
I heard the chick sing in the egg,
and the straw in the mattress grew,
the raspberry cried in the jam.

But I came safe from these shades,
out of the battle-noise gales,
until I reached Slaughter Lad's
and saw there under the moon's eye
a hedgehog milking a jack snipe,
a goat beating a drum in the sky —
I had crossed over the borders of the live.

I walked into his head —
no knife, no healing herb —
helix of a snail's shell,
into a complex corridor.
Prayers of hate, echoes of roars
fell from the faceted walls —
his father's face was carved on the floor.

'I hit him hit him hit him again —
the goose drank the juice of this brain,
I made a pig-trough from his skull
and put his eyes under a hen.
One did not hatch at all,
the other shook and cracked.
Out walked a chicken's claw.

'The claw still sticks in me —
it tortures and exhausts:
contrition runs from my nose,
surgeon, give me peace.'
I refused. And left the place.
I threw away all style and craft,
my heart was ash and chaff,
my soul was a gravel bed —
a naked surgeon, and my patient dead.

6

The one-eyed monk sits,
half prays where millstones turn.
His body comes to life,
a need to travel grinds him up —
a need for pools full of hope,
a need for wells of honey and sweat,
a need for hills where torches burn.

He walks the white-flowered field
looking for a ferny place
clad in sparse purple light
(a foxglove round a bee)
to a mild meadow of sheep,
to soft dark, root of history —
peace to all who walk this way.

But only silence from his bell,
dead butterfly his manuscript
— unfinished, unrevised —
he is addicted to this trip,
this drug called pilgrimage
that kills all dignity and skill
and still's his reason to exist.

And when the monk grows weak,
clumsy, worn, aged —
no more desire to roam,
wanting his bell and page.
But he can no longer illuminate,
has lost the power to pray,
lost his interest in the everyday.

This travel's an enormous act,
a trip all have to take,
and meadows and mountains lure
all who want to escape
with coaxing honey, coaxing kiss,
'Do not search for new things,
do not search for new things'.

I will drown all my books
in that honeyed well
and play like a foal
in the brownest fern.
I will swim in the pool of hope,
I will walk till night in the bright fields.

But in the splendid dark I'll hear
wings of parchment shake and bells weep.

'Bereft of its great poets . . .'

Bereft of its great poets
our old world's in darkness.
The orphans of those masters
offer answers that lack sharpness.

Their books are sadly mildewed —
books that were not flippant —
their lore unjustly *passé*,
though lore of wisdom-drinkers.

I pity the man who must witness the fate of himself,
now that poets are gone, who valued both wisdom and verse:
while their sons retain not one jot of that lore in their heads
old volumes disintegrate, dusty and mouldy, on shelves.

after the Irish of Dáibhí Ó Bruadair

'Pity the man who English lacks . . .'

Pity the man who English lacks
  now turncoat Ormonde's made a come-back.
As I have to live here, I now wish
  to swap my poems for squeaky English.

after the Irish of Dáibhí Ó Bruadair

Inchicore Haiku

My English dam bursts
and out stroll all my bastards.
Irish shakes its head.

No Avail

Suddenly Christ closed his eyes
and the light died inside you.
Mother Church became hard frost
and her incense dropped cold dew.

Now your refuge seems to be
freedom in the world outside —
the song, the crowd, and the dance,
the romance you were denied.

Now you see your brown-eyed prince
waiting with his song and kiss
there in the lost green demesne
in coverts where lovers hid.

But the sneering world turns on rusty cogs,
a middle-aged man is the prince you lost;
the green, lost demesne is sawdust and logs
and the frost of Christ is eternal frost.

A Falling Out

for Pat Boran

That kind of summer's day when music comes
down from the hills and sings in small back-rooms
and half-sets from a century before
batter their complex hobnails on the floor
and long laments in overcoats and caps
draw tears, reluctant from the porter-taps —
that was the kind of day it was, that day
when I forsook the world of earn and pay.
There, on the cobbles of the market square,
where toothless penny ballads rasped the air,
there among spanners, scollops, hones, and pikes,
limp Greyhound cabbage, mending-kits for bikes,
velvet calves in creels, women's overalls,
she shook my hand beside the market stalls.
And there before the coulter of a plough,
aware of all the gifts she could endow,
aware, as women are, of all her powers,
as startling as a bunch of winter flowers,
she tricked from me my childish, sacred vow.

I got to know her lovers one by one:
some saw her in an eclipse of the sun,
some saw her practise magic with strange herbs
and made her opaque alchemies of verbs —
some, for her sake, thought blood her favourite wine,
and some thought spirits helped them to divine
her arcane instincts and, as holy fools,
would chant her words not known to any schools.
Some thought that secret nurture made her grow
and more believed she thrived in public show;
some scattered syntax like the blackthorn snow
in flashy spangles on the mud below

and some, like me, immersed themselves in laws,
for what good are the sparks without the straws?
But none of these sufficed. All through the land
I see the poets in their mad distress —
all favoured rivals? No, but victims, yes.
A creature driven by a savage gland,
she takes, and then dismisses, out of hand,
the men and women that she most does bless.
She does not rest, she does not detumesce.

I leave her by a river on a bed,
a silken landscape underneath her head,
and spread her in her finest courting gown
on a spectacular eiderdown
with painted eyes and rings to catch the light
by the oblivious water overnight.
Only the poets can make her come to life,
the stricken catalyst, who call her wife —
at dawn I give her bed a gentle shove
and amputate the antennae of love
and watch the river carry her away
into the silence of a senseless bay
where light ignores the facets of her rings
and where names are not the names of things.

Mountains, Fall on Us

1

White as squid among the roseate prawns
his fingers placed with prim finesse
the seaweed in a green coiffure
about the diamond ice
and gesticulating back he eyed his work
and pursed, 'It's finished; very nice'.
Outside the Easter air was full of drums
and penitents swayed by
with Christs on catafalques
and one man-fearing man at the café door
blew to him a loud and squeaking kiss.
This brought him back to earth,
back to the Confraternity bands
with their jeering trumpets
in the hooded hostile street,
away from his sea mosaics,
away from his rightful place.
With a handkerchief white-winged
like a seagull in his hands
some waiter kindly dabbed
the distraught mascara from his face.

2

At school, in simple linen, whitest cloth,
just twelve, I played a part and played it well.
Away from gaudy pageants, in the cool hall,
away from the drumming in the Easter air,
from satin swamped in crisp cascades of lace,
static in a *tableau*, I was cast
as John, the most beloved disciple.
Ah, no matadors for me,
no heroes of the Civil War —
not even Father, like a flower in steam,
scarlet and saffron in his kitchen whites,
among the copper and the silver pans —
I had a more fatal and more childish dream.
I had found the perfect part
which gave me scope to love and weep
and not to suffer overmuch,
which let me pose, a statue carved from snow
startling in the green palms.
In my fatal, childish dream I could not know
my cross was on its way, already planed
and dovetailed in some workman's hands.

3

I never picture her as young:
always cut from the blackest stone,
the shine of a cross around her neck
as bright as the superstition in her eyes;
and if I say, 'Woman, look at me, your son!'
she looks beyond my shining hair
and ignores the perfume in the room.
She does not see the message in my face;
I'm just, to her, a list of childish woes.
She stores my real sins in dark recesses
with her lace and clothes.
Her mind rejects according to its means
(her mind that dreams the vital dreams
implanted in a body that breaks down
in its faulty universe
and with it breaks her dreams)
a crystal flower growing on a ledge
that always crumbles into dust, and as the ledge
slips down the crystal flower crumbles
and goes down with the débris,
scintillating, faint. She prays for me.
Her milestones are novenas for the dead.

4

In the University Garden, God, it all goes wrong —
as I sit here in a soul I do not want,
in a person I can't love,
as by a kiosk students kiss.
I had no real plans when I was young,
just slid into this self I have,
not thinking it would be as bad as this.
Although I cannot live another life —
nor do I want to live the other life —
I live this life which has no joy in it,
no lovers — just accomplices.
I sit, pretend to read, but watch instead
the languorous students in the pampas grass
by the dry fountains, as lovely and as distant as
the poets on their plinths dissolving into sand
in the corrosive smoke.
The flowers are tawdry in the dust
like me, a morning dancer coming home
dishevelled after wine and broken by rebuffs,
my face dissolving like the poets,
the smut of night invading my white cuffs.
I'd love a drink, something cold and nice —
ah yes, the honey of Cuarenta y Tres
jostled by its diamond ice!

5

Oh why do we audition for the glamorous roles
and only get to play the corpse?
I have read the Alexandrian Greek,
his drab epistles to his secret flock
(I vowed my life would be more fine than his,
not the constant victim of some boy
and his battening accomplices).
He found refuge in exotic names,
Dimaratos, Dimitrios, Aimilianos, Manoi,
but his real poems told of real pain.
I vowed my life would be more fine than this.

And now I sit forsaken and stood up
in a no-star eating-house,
a one-armed bandit hurdy-gurdying out
the same synthetic notes,
where the floorboards wear their patina of dirt
as tourists wear a fading tan,
as the overhead electric fan
cuts slices from the curdling smoke
and garlic curses clatter in the kitchens.
Not for me the poet's gold *Dimaratos*
stood up and staring at a plastic rose:
I am living now in one of his more real fictions.

6

So here in this no-star eating-house
I have run out of character:
I am not able for the lines.
This John — if he was beloved —
had in him, by the Cross,
in the copper shadow of the moon's eclipse,
seeds planted that would grow
into a forest of Apocalypse;
nothing in my mind fits me for this part
or for any other; even Judas had his role,
his kiss the pivot of the tale,
he was in the script: no Judas no betrayal;
and Peter destined for his anguish
on the Appian Way
where the guilt broke from his brain
and like a living bead of sweat
jumped from his head and formed a Christ
walking into Rome;
and the good thief on the right (or left) hand
was bound for Paradise
and Pilate shuffled off
to a Roman reprimand.
I am not able for their lines.

7

'There is one left,' the mirror says to me,
as I practise the occupation of the lost,
reading the labels on the shelf.
Behind the bottles' shoulders I can see
my prismatic self.
'But who is left? All the parts are cast,
just a scattering of women on the hill,
Magdalene, the Mother, and the rest:
all the roles are filled.'
'There is one left,' say the ice-cubes in my glass,
chirping from the shaking of my hand,
'he got no promise of eternal bliss,
of green oases flaring in the sand.
He hung on the great loneliness
of his forgotten cross
as the other drifted off to Paradise.
He asked for mercy and was snubbed by Christ.'

I feel the mallets smash my thighs.
I order the cheapest possible cigar.
An alternative saviour joins me at the bar.

The Old Catechism

for Jim Downey

Tears, that have been stagnant
for so long,
force their way with burrs of salt
from my blurred eyes,
down my disintegrating face
as I, past fifty, realise
it's certain I shall leave
many songs unsung;
and the poems I have made
(all written out of praise
for you, and all for you)
shall get scant hearing
and that not in your bright lit courts,
but in some *salon de refusé*
where thwarted poets throng.
Tears, when invitations are not sent,
come as easily to the middle-aged
as they do to the very young.

The room where the music comes from
is not far off
but I will open the wrong door
and silence will swish its baton
and all grow still.
I can hear the bullies scoff
as they contemplate the violence
about to be inflicted:
no attempt at wit
through bleeding teeth
now parries the blow;
no logic now forestalls

the boot in the ribs,
the kick in the balls.
Far too late I call on you
whom I dodged and cheated
and whom I always thought
would rescue me
by some *deus ex machina* means;
but now my toes and fingers bleed
crushed by the very gang I sided with:
my compassion's pulped
like a beetle underfoot,
my poems are spiked in their latrines.

And we shall never meet:
I shall have to be content
with a glimmer of gold cloth
as a door closes,
of a sweet light
that the closure changes
into a long and half-dark night;
and even if I draw blinds open
there never shall be day outside,
never again a glimpse of something
that glitters.
The pictures on the wall
will frame a deeper dark,
the hall will be as empty and as stark
as a desecrated tomb.
I shall not be asked to go
where the music is
nor be asked to join
your guests and you
next door in the splendid room.

Why you accept the reputation
foisted on your work
by minds that have to have
a programme and a rule
I shall never know.
You strut, with sheaves of paper,
paying homage with your peers —
a homage you must pay
for interminable years
to your remote dictator:
your reward for keeping to
the strait and narrow way.
It is no major deed,
for, given the advantages you have —
the ambition, charm and guile,
the willing showrooms where you can rehearse,
the widespread agents
who proclaim your craft —
given these, I, too, could create
(but perhaps not choose to live in) such a universe.
They decorate this room
with their mediocre pieties
who never knew the splendour of a mortal sin,
the satisfaction of a fine poem flawed,
the contradictions in a soul
that is always eager to begin
and course, whether an end's in sight or not,
or even achievable.
Impeccably dressed, with perfect pitch
they sing their host's most favourite song.
It is the evening they have worked
and waited for —
but to me an evening that goes on too long.

However. There is a house I've heard of —
where the herbs are always fresh
and where, at last, pain and panic are dismissed,
and you can walk in, take off your aches,
sit down, discard your fear,
and say: 'Hello God. I'm here.'

14 December 1992
10 pm

The Man who Wrote Yeats, the Man who Wrote Mozart

for John B. Keane

In crisp italic, meticulous and signed,
the manuscripts arrived by every post.
From somewhere in the North.
From someone not quite right.
From someone with a perfect hand who wrote,
'"What then?" sang Plato's ghost,
What does it shadow forth?"'
with one word changed in every other line.

I was confronted once again
by a mind which lives by that
intangible, subordinating rule,
the mental scaffolding of which
rests on shifting ground:
the compulsion to believe
what is provably untrue;
and seems to us to be
something not quite right,
something not quite sound.

I could have, very easily, undermined
the props that gave such makebelieve support;
but not so long before I wrote
a piece based on a line
I'd read in Alexander Pope —
so could I now afford
to call his work a fraud
and give the benefit of truth to mine?
If he believed that he had written Yeats
as I believed my poem was mine
he was no sham but simply lacked the art
to make his source opaque

with a flourish of technique.
Or maybe he was mad
and was dancing to a lie,
a dance so furious
that it does not stop when its music does.

And I knew this lie: it is a brake
that holds a frantic flywheel back
which, if it's loosened,
spins the cogs inside the head
at such a frightening rate
it cuts to fragile tangles
and to quivering springs
the fine machinery of the brain;
for I have seen a wounded mind retreat
away from windows that could see the street
when its lie has been exposed
and move to the dead corners of a house
and hide in the remotest room
to where no contradictions come
and an endless talking flows
between it and its cherished lie,
a broken doll in tawdry clothes.
And if anyone intrudes
and tries to comfort and confront
there will be silence in the rooms —
for after contradiction silence comes.

Perhaps he sat there in his northern glen,
in some pub or kitchen, and convinced
an audience and himself
that a poet had arrived;
and so enchanted with the praise,
the adulation that the Irish give
to one they think a scribe,

he brought, with manic, altering pen,
astonished poems of Yeats
before the eyes of equally astonished men.

And in Austria, 1791,
real rustics, in an evening light,
trudge and murmur up a hill
towards the entrance of a gaudy *Schloss*
to stand about a statued yard all night,
obedient, at a total loss,
to suffer music that they cannot grasp
from Franz, the Graf von Walsegg's quill.

'My latest Opus, a quartet
for 'cello, flute, viola, violin,
has got a suave *adagio*, based
(with some refinements)
on a peasant air.
It floats about and *interlaces*, as it were,
all the fabric of the piece,
with its silver thread
above the labour of the strings
that try to reach a semblance of its grace
without ever getting there.'
Thus, in his baroque domain
(Stoppach, Pottschach, Ziegersberg and Klam)
the kindly Count von Walsegg rambles on,
gracious in a gilded chair,
to family and friends;
with all the servants there
admiring in its plush
the German flute he had especially made
and his 'cello, chestnut in its curves,
and the music, glittering on an ornate shelf
in vellum bindings commissioned by the Graf,

immaculately scripted by himself
(black notes like beads of jet,
treble clefs like heads of fern):
Sonata, Trio, and Quartet
by Franz Anton Hoffmeister and François Devienne —
with some notes changed in every other staff.

And yet the Count loved music
(as my fellow-poet loved
every line he ever cribbed).
An adept on the 'cello and the flute,
he kept his court musicians,
copied out whole works by hand,
and paid out gulden by the score;
but like my fellow-poet
the pages that he turned,
the alchemy of quill and nib,
the structures of another man,
the very perfume of the ink
transformed a striving to adore
to a more cunning thing.
Von Walsegg had an audience in thrall
and was not bothered that beyond
the limits of his county and estate
his name was never heard;
he in fact preferred
(to possible exposure and disdain)
the smug comfort of a local fame.
But Death which disregards
all claims and provenance
came into his *ersatz* life
and took his twenty-year-old
Countess off his hands;
and only finest marble,
marble cut like music,

and music that was marble-like
would do to mark his mourning for his wife:
so Johann Martin Fischer,
finest sculptor of his day,
was commissioned — to design
a fitting monument
to guard her bones and honour them,
and to see her soul
safely placed among the saints —
Mozart, to write a requiem.

Till now von Walsegg was content
to re-embroider any trifling cloth
his monies could so easily procure;
but soon, a *Mozart* would present
a great and glittering robe
to wrap in definite remembrance here
his dead wife's soul;
and so at last the Count had found
a work to match his mania
and went on to claim (his alibi a smile)
the magnificent *pastiche*
as his last and greatest tribute to his wife
and took the plaudits as his due
and bowed into the candelabra's glow.
But the snickering musicians knew.
The snickering musicians always know.
Oh the wardrobes we have gone through
to dress our naked minds!
What goods we've cheapened and what suits
we've tried to cover up our tattered clothes,
to patch up every threadbare place
through which sharp wind continually blows
from the cold halls of space.
As Aristotle crippled logic

for two thousand years
and Plato and his minions
cluttered up the sky
with their humming spheres
the convolvoli
of things already done
keep us trapped, like any moon
bound to its sun like a tethered goat
whose grass must finally run out;
and though not at all at ease
in this treadmill heaven,
as we argue from the given to the given
we see as we spin past
other systems, other stars
that we can never visit;
and though taught there's nothing new
underneath the sun,
that there's a limit to the roses
we can breed and cull,
we are not at all at ease
with the insistent notion
of something new underneath the skull.

I, I think, have not succumbed
(not all the time, at any rate)
to von Walsegg's and my fellow-poet's
more cunning and more artless ways
but if others' work had so bedazed their minds,
so made the base of all they wrote —
how much am I bedazed?
How much mine is what I write?
Does the superimposition of a poem
naturalise another's thought
or bend his stray reflections
to the poet's will

as some composers build
partitas on the squeak that's made
as hands slide up guitars?
It is like pouring milk into a stream
high up a hill:
though down it comes some hundred feet
(effervescent over rocks
or lulled to tarns
behind some elbow of grassed turf,
falls, tumbles, runs or slows as smooth
as a dark honey ooze)
and may be called
a rivulet, a runnel or a rill,
it still comes out a stream
that someone poured some milk into
high up a hill.

So, repeatedly seduced and repeatedly annoyed
at being seduced and led
by the odder machinations of the heart,
I try to move outside the human rote
but find myself instead
in landscapes where the plants,
the beasts, are strictly catalogued;
where frightening hybrids melt into the dark
and where language that lacks echoes
strikes discords in the head.
So, fearing a descent
to syntax that ignores
the grammar of our kind,
I try to hew out parables
from the broken torsos that I find.

But I am not contented in my mind.

Sibelius in Silence

for Angela Liston

To have intricacies of lakes and forests,
harbours, hills, and inlets given —
and none of these with a name;
then to have posited nomads straggling
from the barricading Urals
bearing on their backs and horses
children, language, and utensils,
gods and legends;
then to have brought all these together,
yeast to the thawing mud —
this was to make in the Green Gold of the North
an ethnic and enduring bread.

They settled where their dead
were buried and gave names
to every hill and harbour,
names that might become unspoken
but would forever whisper 'Not yours'
to mapping strangers;
their dead became the land they lived on,
became the very lakes and corries,
the very myths and shadows that live
inside the birch and pine tree;
their dead sprung up in grains and berries
nourishing their offspring
that inhabited the cold expanses.
They sowed their gods in caves and hillsides,
gods that might become forgotten
but would forever whisper 'Go home'
to dreaming strangers.

After the land is first immersed
in language, gods, and legends,

sown with blood and bodies,
whatever strangers come and conquer
and stand upon the hills at evening
(for even planters tend to meditation)
they will sense they are not wanted here;
for the wind, the old, old voices
moulding ice and snowdrifts
into Arctic intimations of the shapes,
now quite unhuman, they possess
in a dead and parallel present,
will tell them:
'You are not ours, you are not wanted,'
and the lake, the pine, the birch tree,
the very slope and curve of mountain,
all will say the same:
'The name you call us by is not our name.'

Whoever comes and conquers —
from the first flake of fish eaten,
from the first crumb of bread taken
in this place —
blood in water and in ground
transubstantiates that race
and performs an altering justice;
its homeland becomes myth;
its very customs, clothing, accent
(if not language) change
and now are woven
from other soils and other souls
in this intricate biosphere.
It is not wanted here
nor loved at home;
it watches rivers wash
its labels from their banks
contemptuously to sea,

watches names it put on hills
detach themselves and doggedly slide down
a valley of unwanted nouns.
It sits inside its palisade
and sees its gods move out of reach
and fade
before the bright gods of the older race,
its children's mouths ringed purple
with their speech.
When I was young I did not know their language.
I visited the inns of Babel
where old and young drank mugs of syntax
that turned on tongues and hands to music,
where men at beer-ringed counters
told me their melodious open secrets
and I held up identity papers
and said, 'I *do* belong: this *is* my country',
and they let me join their ranks —
for part of me indeed throughout the centuries
had become this race's;
and although my origins still slunk
some thousand years away
in heavily guarded strong-rooms in my head
their edges had the tint,
had absorbed the purple hue
that revealed I ate
the berries that the conquered grew;
all this (papers, costume, customs,
fibre transformed and muscles
and my longing to belong)
was negated by my voice,
my traitor larynx
that then could never frame
their simplest proverb
or sing their simplest song —

but courtesy is not acceptance
so I left the friendly inns
and walked into the dark,
landmarks all around me
hinting at the road,
and a calvary of signposts
on which strange names were shown
that pointed out the way
but not the way home.

Blacker than the blackest swans are,
all my life their mythic figures
clothed in insistent rhythms
have pursued me and made me anxious,
called my name, and demanded answers:
and I listened. And I answered.
Music was my language, so I gave them my music;
and the land drank in my music.
Caught at school in webs of grammar
which still at night enmesh my face,
I had no tongue in the land I came from
but at first, at best, a stammer;
but the fluency I sought I found
in the speech that underlies my music.
The land took me in her embrace;
I wed the land and dreamed her freedom
somehow coalesced and marched *maestoso*
out through the hatchings of my music-sheets.
But the people heard the real programme:
the *crescendi* of shells in the air
and their climax in the streets.

'Alcohol's a cunning beast.
It fools the doctor and the priest,

it fools the clever and the sane —
but not the liver or the brain.'
Idle verses, so I thought
that someone, doodling, idly makes.
But now blood breaks like snowflakes
from my brothers' nostrils
and my hand shakes.
I gave everything I could:
music, speeches, pat harangues;
intellectualised the fight
and, *tremblando*, wept *adagios*, wrung my hands —
in short, spilled every drink but blood.
Autumn breaks its rainbows
along the staggering trees
and my hand quivers.
Into my room across my music-sheets
sail black swans on blacker rivers.

They say my music weeps for the days
when my people ate the bark from trees
because all crops had failed.
Music disdains such theories:
I offer you here cold, pure water —
as against the ten-course tone-poems,
the indigestible Mahlerian feasts;
as against the cocktails' many hues,
all liquors crammed in one glass —
pure, cold water is what I offer.
Composed, I am conducting. It is my
fourth symphony, third movement and,
as my baton tries to make the music keep
to the key of C sharp minor,
vodka ebbs in tremors from my hand
and at the ragged corner of my eye
a raven flies through the concert hall

and I find a self saying to myself,
'It was the deer that stripped the trees,
not the people at all.'
Two flutes grapple with an ice-cold note
until the 'cello takes command.
As the audience's hiss escapes
splinters of birch-bark stick in my throat.

And now, because I made such strict demands
upon my art, I must dismiss such music as intrudes
on me as I conceal my shaking hands.
No loss indeed — it's now quite trivial and crude;
no more legends come out of the northern lands,
no more Virgins of the Air, no more black swans,
no more seamless symphonies project themselves.
I take down a book of poetry from my shelves
to share with my children's children the old store
of verses that this green-gold land reveres
(I speak their native language fluently
but when excited lapse into my planters' tongue).
You may think thirty years of silence far too long
but some composers now about should have learnt from me
that silence would have graced the world far more
than their gutting and dismembering of song.
And that which was part of me has not left me yet —
however etherialised, I still know when it's there.
I get up at odd hours of the night
or snap from a doze deep in a chair;
I shuffle to the radio, switch on the set,
and pluck, as I did before, *Finlandia* out of the air.

He'll to the Moors

for Paul Murray, OP

Since 'tis not to be had at home,
She'll travel to a martyrdom:
No home for hers confesses she
But where she may a martyr be.
She'll to the Moors, and trade with them
For this unvalued diadem.

— Richard Crashaw,
'*A Hymn to the Name and Honour*
of the Admirable Saint Teresa',
1646

Though many live by logic
no one dies for it.
Ptolemaic, Euclidean schemes
impel no martyrs to stake
or fiery pit:
what we die for are our dreams . . . .
Such words, or similar, come to haunt me
now in my old age, that never came
when I was young and, idling with a lute,
I matched light love-songs to ephemeral tunes
and laughed with kings and sons of kings and chased
the finest of all game, women old and young,
brought them down like quail in nets, and then
devoured their tender parts and left their wings
impaled on thorns of shame. But one, most plump,
most pious, and most pure, escaped all snares;
one, the more her pride and body seemed
so given to good works and God, the more
desperate I was to bring her down.

Anger and desire became a cloud that,
anvil-headed, threatened to explode

in purple thunder on her head till one black day
she had acceded at long last to my request,
my rabid importuning. I had done my best,
with eyes and songs, with roses in her missal pressed,
to intimate to her how much I was obsessed
by her fine shape that moved with such a sexual zest,
it seemed, on Sundays. She ignored each wild behest
and went escorted always, putting me to test
as I could see her limbs, no matter how she dressed,
move in copper grandeur deep in their woven nest.
No flick of fan, no chin tipped up in scorn, could wrest
from me the eagerness to finalise my quest.
And then a letter came: I was to be her guest.

Her eyes were calm. No passion showed as she undressed
like some Salomé; but, distant and unimpressed,
she stood in a pool of drapes. Only a light vest
now hid the body I had vowed would be caressed.
She pulled the cloth aside: 'I grant you your request.'
Now, I who thought that I could find some kind of rest,
could vent some kind of anger on a woman's breast,
saw, putrid, cratered, flaking like an old wasp's nest,
that cancer which, destroying part, disfigures all the rest
(that does not only body, but also soul, digest)
and on the ruin of once fine flesh, God's last jest,
a nipple standing sentinel on its black crest.

Such shocks the soul can take, and music helps:
I now gave up my lust and set myself
instead to set small lyrics to small tunes
hammering the sight of that decaying breast
into the mother-of-pearl frets. I stayed
indoors, drugged by folksong, hummed the airs
the common sang, refined the words and, almost
as a penance, wrote poetry: small songs

that glittered like false jewels and like them
unreal; and they did not tell the truth
like mad composers who, back in daylight
for a while out of their frightful dark,
write happy dances in which no terror
is discerned. These pastimes kept my mind
compartmentalised until one day
in that silence, in that minute pause,
between one note of music and the next,
there came a suspension of all laws:
I saw the great Cross with its mocking text
stained like old timber with spilt blood
from the tortured face of my sad Christ,
saw His kingdom and its cause —
Christ's kingdom at the corner of my eye.
Also in that silence, that short time,
the vision vanished. I did what I could
to persuade myself that I was tired,
that the apparition of the holy wood
was a trick of eyesight. But for two days more
that broken body came and hung,
an instant just, above my bedroom floor
like a carcass on a butcher's hook,
the weight of all the world trying to tear
the ripped hands from the iron nails,
pulling it towards the centre of the earth
as if bestraddled by the universe;
and in that silence, that short time, my heart shook.

I gave my reluctant self to many schemes:
teach heathens Christ's essential truths
or bid for martyrdom among those hordes?
But, illiterate, with my few lyric lines,
was not equipped to teach the word of Christ
and so I learnt Latin, Hebrew, Arabic,

that I could now convince those lost,
that could not see through the perfect crystal
of my faith; begged from kings and sons of kings
funds for colleges, for missionary priests,
and with frustration cried in church;

as standard took St Francis, wore coarse cloth,
became a dead man to my children and my wife;
followed on pilgrimage my soul, that had set out
to Santiago, Montserrat, Rocamadour;
came home and with frustration cried in church
and wrote the first of many million words
and faced the mockery of Palma's streets,
neither cleric nor courtier, nor priest;
at home, but celibate, in a makeshift cell,
the sneers of servants burning in my ears.

To teach me Arabic I bought a slave.
He slandered Christ.
I whipped this Moor until he bled
and for mercy cried.
And then this Moor he tried
to kill me with a knife,
so I had him locked away
for three nights
and I went on retreat
praying for advice
but in my cell's darkness
I saw no light.
Home, and found the Moor
had taken his own life:
a rope around his neck,
instead of the Cross of Christ.

So I plunged into debates with scholars,
Hebrews, Moors, hiding myself in logic,
mistaking texts and tracts for real faith
and wrote and wrote my many million words;
and then, for quiet, found a cave on Randa
but found no quiet there: instead I found
the form and order of my future books,
conceived *Ars Magna*, *Ars General* —
a system bound with logic like fine steel,
a mathematic system, to supply
all answers to all questions, whether they
came from the field of Natural Science
or from Theology's highest planes
or from Metaphysics' maze:
I had infallibility ensnared
and ordered on the written page.
And now the kings and sons of kings
had built my school at Miramar
to study Arabic and the Moorish mind
and I had audience with the Pope in Rome
and confounded heathen scholars in debate.

They said: 'Who knows God's hundredth name
must know all things.'
And, further, that mention of this name
must untune the Universe
and leave its polished timber cracked,
entangled in a mesh of strings.
But read, I said, and hear:
'I have walked in lonely places,
have battled with neglected books;
from Chaldean and Egyptian sleep I have woken
every symbol, every token,
that concealed His hundredth name.
I have not left this hundredth name unsaid,

yet there is no rush of knowledge to my head;
I have not left the hundred names of God unspoken
yet the earth's still here, the ranks of stars unbroken.'

So with such logic armed I pleaded with the Pope
to send real armour to the Holy Land;
but, diplomatic then, the Papal ear
decided with Roman wisdom not to hear
but gave me licence to go forth and preach
the Christian message in Tunisia.
But, at Genoa, just about to sail,
my logic left me and my courage failed;
and so to monasteries again,
flirting with the priesthood, in the hope
the chrism of some order would direct my hand.
At 'Veni Creator Spiritus', among Dominicans
I wept, and on the ceiling, a small light
that seemed a star, looked down on me and said:
'Within this order you will find salvation.'
I begged the habit of St Dominic
but, diplomatic too, the Prior refused,
and I went to the Franciscans, there to find
small welcome and no solace for my mind.
My logic, tottering, misled me like the light:
without St Francis all my books would die,
without St Dominic my soul's damnation
was assured: they offered me the Host;
my head was whipped aside and a syllogistic voice
said: 'Take this Host and your soul in sin is lost
but your books will live as long as logic lasts.'
I lay down on the floor and took the Host
so lightly did I weigh my soul
against *Ars Magna, Ars General*.

And so to Tunis, to debate again
with scholars, who so kindly, so urbane,
would follow the esoteric, the abstruse,
for hours; become (in argument) heretical,
would see the flaws in Islam's faith,
and when I showed them proof beyond a doubt
that Christ was God, they would agree
and drink my coffee and mint tea,
but when *muezzins* called to prayer,
mosque-bound, they hurried out,
still Mohammedans to the core . . . .
Then, thinking 'Christ is with the people in the street'
among the many damned misguided souls,
I preached Him in the market and the souk
and got no converts there, for all my pains,
but showers of curses and of stones;
condemned to death and then reprieved;
dragged to a ship and sent to banishment
again I begged the Vatican for aid
but Rome would countenance no new Crusade.
I, starved of solutions that eluded me,
among Franciscans found a little peace.

And I, Ramon, began *El Desconhort*,
my poem of despair: ignored by Court
and Vatican, my college and my books
reduced to rubble;
I, who in this century of ours,
produced the finest verse
and out of chaos came to make
love, logic, letters — all for Christ's sake
(and helped explain that Christ)
got scant pleasure for my trouble . . . .

He now no longer wished to live, but die,
and catch, by any means at all,
the peoples' and God's eye
(as poets, when no longer breathed on,
by the muses' breath).
In Tunisia he was stoned to death.